I0521107

New Beginnings Now

How to be Free From Brokenness

Kanisha Bernice

New Beginnings Now: How to be Free From Brokenness

By Kanisha Bernice

Copyright © 2025 Kanisha Bernice

All rights reserved. No part of this publication may be reproduced, stored in a retrieval system, distributed, or transmitted in any form, or by any means — electronic, mechanical, photocopying, scanning, uploading, recording, or otherwise — without the prior written permission of the author and publisher, except as permitted under US copyright law. If you would like permission to use material from this publication, please contact KB Publishing.

Scripture quotations taken from The Holy Bible, New International Version® NIV® Copyright© 1973, 1978, 1984, 2011 by Biblica, Inc. ® Used by permission. All rights reserved worldwide.

First Edition

Cover Design by Cameron Hagler

Edited by Olivia Morgan

ISBN: 979-8-9931187-0-3

Printed in the US

KB Publishing

Gaffney, South Carolina

Kbfowler11@gmail.com

This book is dedicated to DreamGirls Ministry, a ministry that is empowering girls to achieve their dreams. Girls all over the world can dream big things, believe in themselves and achieve anything they set their mind to. I pray this book will reach as many DreamGirls as possible, allowing them to experience a new mindset, a new attitude, and new behaviors. If you are a girl, lady, or woman anywhere in the world, you are considered a DreamGirl. I dedicate this book to you and the dreams, goals, and aspirations that live in your heart. Your dreams are possible.

CONTENTS

ACKNOWLEDGMENTS

As a little girl with big dreams, goals, and aspirations, there is one person that always remained constant in my life and I want to acknowledge her as a foundational pillar that helped me get to where I am today – my mom. My mom has supported and encouraged me through multiple seasons of life. When things were challenging in our relationship, she was there for me. Although there were plenty of struggles that I didn't share with her, I know she was praying for me. She has always wanted the best for me and the love she provides could never be repaid. I wouldn't be the woman I am today if it weren't for her strength, her story, and her grace. I love you, Mom. Thank you for being a phenomenal woman.

I also want to acknowledge two sweet friends who were with me during these seasons of hardship that I write about in this book - Lovetta Walton and Stephanie Vernon. You two are the best friends I didn't know I needed. Lovetta, when I met you, we instantly connected over our passion for ministry and non profit organizations. God has given me a *new beginning* while you believe and achieve your *stellar beginning*. Stephanie, you've been my prayer warrior, my partner in ministry, and friend for over 11 years. When my heart was broken, you covered me. You held me when I cried and lifted my spirit when I was down. Words can't describe what the two of you mean to me. Our friendship is encouraging, uplifting, and sweet. I am extremely thankful that God placed both of you in my life. It's more than a friendship, it's a Christ-centered connection. I love you to the moon and back!

INTRODUCTION

Dear God, give me a new beginning. I don't want to continue living life this way. I'm hurting and I don't want to hurt. I'm broken and I want to be whole. I want to be happy. I surrender my life to you. You can have everything. I just want you.

As a young woman, desperately searching for someone to love me, I reached my breaking point when the guy I was dating left me and broke my heart. I thought he was the one. He said we were going to get married. But I guess he changed his mind because he left and I was broken. After we broke up, I went to the bar and met a new guy, but because of my pain, I couldn't pretend like I was okay. I didn't want to run to another relationship and ignore how I felt. I wanted to process everything I was feeling and heal. It felt like the heartbreak was a wake up call and I was reminded that I can have better. So I pressed into God and found exactly what I was looking for and more. This isn't another typical story about a broken girl searching for healing. This is a story of a girl with big dreams, who wanted to achieve her dreams, and healing was simply part of her journey. My biggest dreams came true when I healed my heart. When I surrendered everything, and established a true relationship with Jesus, I overcame limiting beliefs that said I wasn't good enough or I can't do that. I found a firm foundation in Christ that told me I'm more than a conqueror and I can do all things in Christ who strengthens me. I thought my life was over when my heart got broken, but it was just the beginning.

As a mentor and coach with DreamGirls Ministry, I've empowered many young girls as they experience a healing journey of their own. Now, I'm going to lead you on a beautiful journey out of brokenness and into a place of healing and wholeness. This journey will take you to a place that is perfect for you to grow closer with your walk with Christ and understand yourself better. As you read each chapter and apply the lessons, your life will grow and you'll see things change. You will experience a new beginning.

New Beginnings is more than just a catchy phrase. It's a journey to change - change your mindset, beliefs and attitudes. It's a movement that reminds you that you can experience change whenever you want to. When you've been in the dark hole, you can wake up and decide that you want to do things differently. You can let go of the past and move forward in life. You can do whatever you want to do. There is nothing holding you down and nothing standing in your way. You can be new, right now. If you want to be a business owner, or find a new job and move to a different city, all of that is possible. If you are a believer of Christ, you know how to take delight in The Lord and He will give you the desires of your heart.

The principles and lessons within this book have helped many people walk through the darkest and most painful parts of their life and into the brightest and most amazing parts. There is a beautiful reward at the end of this journey. It's a reward that comes after you receive God's healing and wholeness.

Before we begin, I want to invite the spirit of curiosity into your space. Give yourself permission to be yourself and permission to feel what you feel. When you hear things you've never heard before and see things you've never seen before, ask questions before you cancel and cast it away. Allow your spirit to align together with mine. My prayer is that we will be of one accord as I write and you read. Although I'm not sitting beside you, the goal is that we will have a connection through each word on each page and you will understand the message of what I'm trying to portray.

Let the Journey Begin

If any man be in Christ, he is a new creation. The old is gone, the new is here. 1 Corinthians 5:17 KJV

This scripture reveals that we can be new in Christ. While on this journey you will uncover pieces of yourself that may be buried deep within your heart. Some things that God wants to make new are your mindsets, beliefs and attitudes. These things may not be living on the surface, but the Spirit of God will take a deep dive into your heart and will reveal these things to you.

He will reveal the truth about who you are and what you're purposed on this earth to do. You are royalty. A child of the King. God is our loving father that wants to have a personal relationship with you. Are you ready to go to a deeper level within your relationship with him? Even if you've been a Christian all your life and you know a lot about God, there is so much more He wants to reveal. Will you open your heart to receive it?

As I think about deep relationships, I think about seeds and roots. Roots must grow deep before a seed can grow out of the ground. When the seed for a tree is planted, it takes a while to grow and become what it's meant to be. If you were to consider your life as a garden, the seeds that were planted in you when you were a kid may take years to become fully grown. Some seeds will become trees, some will become flowers, some will become plants. All of which can be colorful, vibrant and thriving – or they can be rotten, damaged and unfruitful. God wants every part of you to thrive. When you don't allow God to have full access to your heart, it is impossible to blossom the way He wants you to blossom. The good news is, it's not too late for God to start or finish His work. If you're reading this book, I believe you've walked into a divine set up that will allow God to soften your heart and let Him have full access. This will be your journey to experience the life that you've always wanted to achieve.

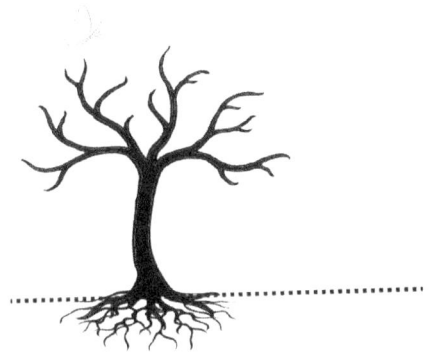

Journey
through
Brokenness

IDENTIFYING WHAT IS BROKEN

Before the sun rises in the morning, the darkest part of the night lingers on the earth.

If you've ever woken up early to watch the sunrise, you understand how dark the night is, but as soon as the sun breaks through the barriers of the atmosphere, you can see the shift from dark to light. Even on cloudy days when the sun isn't shining, the evidence of light behind the clouds proves that the sun has risen.

The journey through brokenness is like the sun rising early in the morning. In our darkest hour - when things are painful, overwhelming and sad - if we cling to the hope and aspirations of a new beginning, the light will come. Darkness will be overpowered and the sun will shine bright into every area of our life.

This metaphor can be true for many seasons - seasons of grief like losing a parent or loved one, depression after a breakup, financial hardship, trouble with school, work, and other things. No matter the cause of your brokenness, your light will come if you press through the darkness and believe for greater. Breakthrough is possible. It may take a while, but it will come.

Everyone experiences brokenness at least once in their life and I would argue the impact increases right before breakthrough. A season of brokenness is a short period of time where things are uncomfortable, and a lot of your deep-rooted pain comes to the surface. In this season, you can make healthy choices and process your feelings, identify issues of your heart, and get connected to your spirit – or you can make unhealthy choices and bottle your emotions, run from your pain and disconnect from life.

When my heart was broken, I was at my lowest point, one of the darkest places I had ever been, but God told me I was strong enough to get through it. I felt like my life was breaking into a million pieces, but instead of running away from the pain, I stayed. I wanted to leave and find something to take the pain away, but I knew that wouldn't be a permanent solution. Another relationship wouldn't heal me. Another late night at the club or the bar wouldn't change the way I felt. I wanted to heal and experience the wholeness I had heard so many people talk about. Deeper connection with Jesus Christ was the only thing that would do that. I learned how to identify the things in my life that were broken and process my pain. I didn't know it then, but my mindsets and my attitudes were broken. My beliefs were broken. I thought I had a good relationship with God, but to experience the things I was asking for, I had to do things I wasn't used to doing, like sitting quietly with God, learning how to slow down, and implementing deep breathing to capture my thoughts. It was different and it felt strange in the beginning, but it helped me identify the things that weren't working – the broken things.

In order to identify the things that are broken in your heart, it requires you to be real and honest. Shallow and superficial friendships shouldn't be allowed. You need friends that will call you out when you're walking away from God and hold you accountable when you want to run from your pain. If you want to be free from the pain, you have to learn the importance of compassion and sitting with your emotions. Don't run, don't hide your heart; open yourself up and be vulnerable. Be vulnerable with God, with yourself, and with your friends. Vulnerability leads to healing. One of the most honest things you can do is open your heart and share your feelings, wants, and needs. That takes courage.

Many people don't choose to do this because they don't trust others. That's understandable, but as you walk through this journey, you have to learn who you can trust and who you can't. Some people aren't safe. Find the people that truly care about you and want you to experience the life that God has for you. Find the people with a good heart and good intentions. If you're in a season where you don't have that, learn how to give it to yourself and wait for God to bring you true friends.

When I was a little girl, I remember going to the store with my dad and while walking, I asked him a simple question, "Do you love me?" His response was really strange for a 6 year old. Initially, I thought it was rude, but as an adult, I understand what he was trying to say. He replied, "Do you love yourself?" I said "Yes," and he said, "That's all that matters."

I believe my dad was trying to teach me a valuable lesson. This lesson doesn't apply to every situation, but it applies here when it comes to healing. It's okay to give yourself the gift of love. With things like firm boundaries, clear expectations, truth and honesty, forgiveness, trust, compassion, and empathy – this is the best way to love yourself. This isn't prideful or egotistical – it's healthy. Love becomes unhealthy when it's full of selfishness, revenge, fear, unforgiveness, and lack of empathy.

When love lives in the heart, it flows easily to other people. When brokenness and pain live in the heart, that is what flows to other people. The reference of the heart is used to acknowledge the internal part of you. Your heart is also known as your spirit, or your subconscious mind. It carries your desires, your beliefs, and your dreams. Proverbs 4:23 says to guard your heart, for everything you do flows from it. Light and darkness cannot coexist. One will always overpower the other. When God's love is in your heart, brokenness cannot stay there. Anytime your heart is broken, let God's love take the pain away.

When situations cause your heart to break, it's typically because your expectations and desires weren't met. Broken hearts don't always mean you're sad, sometimes your broken heart causes you to be mean and disrespectful to others. A broken heart will cause you to stop dreaming and believing that anything good can happen. Many people are living with a broken heart and don't realize it. They're carrying pain that has turned to bitterness. They're carrying unforgiveness that has turned to hatred. All of this is a result of expectations and desires that weren't met.

Their heart is broken and they're dealing with pain they haven't released. They won't reveal it to God. Instead they're pretending like everything is fine when emotionally and mentally they are disconnected and dissociated. That's how I was. I smiled, I pretended, and I kept everything to myself for years. I was bound emotionally and mentally. I wanted to be free but I didn't know how.

When I started this journey with the Lord, God taught me how to process the issues of my heart. He taught me how to understand and listen to my heart. God needed to break attitudes, mindsets, and behaviors out of me, but he couldn't do any of that until I surrendered it all to Him and learned to be real about how I felt.

The journey that followed as I began to pick up the pieces of my life was strategically orchestrated by God. I call it a journey because that's what each day felt like. I wanted to heal from the pain of my most recent relationship, but I didn't know the steps on how to do that. I was trusting God and refusing to use another relationship to cover up my pain.

The breakup was ugly. Although the relationship didn't please God, I begged Him to bring that guy back into my life. God said no. It was time to heal. I knew I wanted a marriage that honored the Lord, so I made the decision to stay single and begin my healing journey. While doing so, I discovered a relationship with someone far greater than any guy – Jesus.

In 2018, as I started my healing journey, I learned how to

manage the things that were broken in me. What started as giving my heart to the wrong guy ended in giving my heart to someone better. I gave my heart to God and that was the best thing I ever did.

Your heart is your identity. It's who you are. Literally, every piece of you lives in your heart - the good things, the bad things, the light and the darkness. When you have a true relationship with God, you can talk with Him daily. You can share things that make sense and things that don't make sense, things that go well and things that don't go well. God wants to be a part of it all and you have to invite Him into each area of our life. You do that through prayer and conversation, spending time with Him, journaling, writing and doing thing you're talented to do. God is a spirit and He will connect with your spirit anytime you ask Him to come in.

CORE OF YOUR HEART

"Above all else, guard your heart, for everything you do flows from it."
Proverbs 4:23 NIV

The core, or root, of your heart will always be the reason for your actions. When you understand your heart, you will understand why you do what you do. The heart holds your internal beliefs and beliefs guide you. Many times people desire to change without fully understanding themselves. They aren't aware of their personality, their style or the quirky things that make them *them*. Have you ever noticed the behaviors that are automatic to you? It's like an instant reflex. It's something you do without thinking about it.

Think about the last time you ordered a cup of coffee, hot chocolate, or hot tea. The warm cup rests against your fingers and you can feel the heat as you place the cup near your mouth. You take a few moments to blow, then test the heat with a small sip. You can't take a large gulp because you know it's extremely hot. You understand this process all too well; you don't have to think about it because it's automatic.

Other automatic processes include brushing your teeth, tying your shoes, and putting clothes on. You don't have to think about those steps - you just do it. You know it's important and unless there is a physical obstacle preventing you from doing those things, you do it naturally. The way you do it may change over time, but the process itself doesn't change. For an example, you may be accustomed to rushing to put clothes on and running out the door to start your day. Over time, you may change and slow down. As you put your clothes on, you iron your shirt and pants, you make sure your jewelry and accessories match the fit, and spray cologne or perfume which adds a pleasant aroma. The process of putting clothes on didn't change, but you adapted and adjusted the way you do it. You didn't have to think about how to wear your shirt or which leg goes inside your pants first. You know how to put clothes on. You've been doing it every day, your whole life. But one day you may wake up and realize, you don't want to wear the same things you've been wearing all year. You want to wear different colors, different styles and different sizes.

Without realizing it, your beliefs have created patterns that govern your life. This is true for both healthy and unhealthy patterns in your life. A pattern is a routine, action, or habit that is completed daily without you having to think about it. It's the simple things you always do around your home, in your bedroom, in your car, with your friends etc. Some patterns are hidden and you don't realize that you do that. Others are known and it's clear that you do it. Similar to a good habit or a bad habit, you have to identify what it is and be intentional about breaking it if you want to stop doing it.

When I was growing up, I always left my dinner plate on the table. As soon as I was done eating, I would get up and go do something else, forgetting that I never took my plate to the kitchen sink. Constantly, my mom would remind me to pick up my plate and clean up after myself. When I moved out and started living by myself, I realized that I still struggled with leaving my plate on the table. I would notice it 30 minutes or an hour after I had eaten and then I would go back and clean it up. This small pattern that my mom always told me about had followed me into my adult life. Once I realized that was an issue, I made an intentional effort to change it. Although my mom corrected this behavior multiple times when I was growing up, I didn't think an empty plate on the table was that big of a deal. As an adult I understand differently. Change didn't happen until I understood the issue. We don't change bad habits until we see the issue as an issue.

The majority of your bad habits are things you have grown up doing. It's the way you have always lived and because of that, maybe you don't realize that it's harming you or affecting your life. It's hidden. Others may see it as a problem, but you don't. Why fix something that isn't broken, right? Wrong. That's a poor mindset to have. Although something isn't broken, it doesn't mean it's helping you thrive. You have to ask yourself: do I want to survive life barely making it, or do I want to thrive going above and beyond achieving success in all areas of my life? The best way to thrive is to search your heart and allow God to reveal the hidden things that cause you harm.

It's Deeper Than That

Have you ever seen a tree that stood eight feet or even ten feet tall? I have trees taller than this in my yard. They are huge. I believe one of them is a pecan tree but it is too tall to collect the harvest. I always see squirrels in the tree and rotten pecan shells on the ground. Although I'm not sure what type of tree it is, the only way pecan shells would be lying on the ground is if the tree were producing pecans. The proof is in the product. When I think about my actions, I think about trees, and the fruit it produces. If I enjoy the fruit, my goal is to make sure that tree is healthy and sustained. If I don't enjoy the fruit, I aim to uproot and destroy the tree.

A tree is planted by a seed and its roots are established underneath the surface before it grows above the surface. If there are things in your life that you wish you could change, ask yourself, what seeds are planted deep within your heart? Don't put your attention on the actions. The real issue is deeper than that.

When a tree is damaged and needs to be cut down, a true gardener will use specific tools to dig, expose, and remove the roots. God is the gardener of your heart. He wants to expose the unhealthy things that are leading to unhealthy decisions. When God does this, you'll understand where it came from, why you do it and how to change it. This process may take years to accomplish. Uprooting unhealthy mindsets, beliefs, and patterns and replacing them with healthy ones is not a quick journey. But God is patient and gentle. He is not in a rush with your journey. He doesn't get angry with your choices. He loves you and, according to First Corinthians 13, love is patient and kind, and it doesn't keep a record of wrong. He sees the big picture and He understands the things that live below the surface – the root issues within your heart.

God understands you. He sees you. He knows what you have been through, are going through, and will go through in the future. Your past experiences are at the root of your current decisions. Your beliefs, your thought processes, and your decision-making skills make you who you are. All of those things live in your heart. From the way you curl your hair to the way you do your nails, these things help shape your personality. From the secrets you disclose to the pain and heartbreak you withhold, these things live in the hidden compartments that you forgot or didn't know existed.

When you approach matters of the heart with curiosity and compassion, you give yourself permission to release everything that's been breaking you on the inside. Even if you feel fine, there could be brokenness in your heart, and your heart wants to be free.

Before I understood this principle, I went through many heartbreaking relationships without taking time to process the emotions I was carrying. Toxic behaviors from men seemed normal to me because I was disconnected from my heart and unbothered by situations that happened. Simply put, I didn't care. I didn't want to care. I wanted to pretend like nothing bad happened because that made it easier to ignore and forget the painful things. I told myself not to think about the sexual, verbal and mental abuse, that way it couldn't affect me. I

14

pushed all those things to the back of my mind and tried to forget that it happened. When I asked the guy to stop because he was hurting me, but he continued to force his body on my body, I got through that moment and never talked about it again.

I went from relationship to relationship, looking for fulfillment, but instead I found different men, with the same behaviors - liars, manipulators, and abusers. It was a toxic pattern that I became used to. Finding a new boyfriend as soon as one relationship ended was an automatic process because that was the only way I could continue to numb the pain. I didn't want to be still. I didn't want to be quiet. Anytime I did that, the thoughts found a way to come back to my head. Although it was unhealthy, it felt natural because after multiple years of avoiding pain, I became good at it. When I surrendered my heart to God, He revealed these mindsets that were leading me down the path of brokenness. I reached a breaking point where I was miserable and I no longer wanted to be. I didn't realize I was storing these painful memories within my heart. I was trying to deal with it the best way I knew how, but these things were leading to my actions. As God and I began to walk the path of healing, He took me to the beginning where it all began.

I graduated college in 2015 with a dream to work in ministry. Honestly, it was more than a dream. It was a calling that I felt on the inside of me. I felt it so strong, I knew it was from God. Therefore, I didn't apply to many traditional jobs. I launched DreamGirls Ministry in 2014 with a focus to help teen girls achieve their dreams. As a 23-year-old graduate, new to the professional world, my desire was for this nonprofit organization to soar and instantly take off.

I had a part time job and this unrealistic dream. The dream consisted of helping others, being a travel writer, and being financially stable. Although my intentions were good, the reality of my dreams were so far away and my heart was a little broken because of it. I couldn't understand how something I believed in so strongly would take so long to accomplish. Since this is what God told me to do, why couldn't other people see the vision God gave me? Maybe I had unrealistic expectations with life or maybe I expected things to be easy, but all of this led to disconnection and distance with God.

I served in ministry, danced, and sang in the choir, but I needed to spend time at the altar and allow God to fill my heart. I was trying to be obedient to the vision God gave me without proper understanding or clarity on my purpose. My prayer life was weak, and so was my faith. I was frustrated with results from events and ministry. On top of everything, I didn't know the importance of running to God and sharing this truth with Him. I felt like I was all alone, so I held it in and kept everything to myself. Although my emotions were overwhelming, I smiled and said "I'm fine." This was the only way I knew to manage my pain.

God understood all of this. God saw me in moments where no one else saw me. He saw me hurting. He saw my broken heart. When I started dating a guy that was 19 years older than me, He knew that was the way I managed my pain.

Two months after graduation, I met a guy who was handsome, charming, and addictive. When we first met, we spent a lot of time talking on the phone. For hours, all throughout the day, we talked. Although he was 19 years older than me, he was cool and fun to be around. My parents didn't know I was dating him, so basically, I was sneaking around with him. I knew the relationship wasn't serious, and I thought it was harmless to be his friend. This was supposed to be my time to focus on ministry and go all in with my dreams. I didn't think a random guy would get me off track.

I was wrong.

He was verbally abusive and was good at covering it up. He lied and manipulated to get what he wanted. He was controlling. I was defiant. I hated it when people told me what to do. We argued and fought all the time. He never used his hands; he used his words. His words left bruises that affected the way I saw myself even years after we broke up. The whole time we dated it was like a rollercoaster full of break ups and getting back together, arguments, disrespectful comments, and different forms of abuse. I stayed in that relationship when there were clear signs of unhappiness and mistreatment.

Once this relationship ended, I found another one. Guess what? The new guy was just like the old guy. He was older than me. He lied, manipulated, and abused me. At this point, I was really good at numbing the pain and I found comfort in the chaos. For two years we dated, lived together, and tried to have a normal relationship. The fights weren't as bad, but the relationship had no substance. Eventually, that relationship ended and I found another one. This is what I mean by relationship after relationship; it was a cycle of brokenness – a pattern that I knew was toxic, but didn't know how to change.

I never took time to breathe or release anything. I was holding on to so much and I held it until I hit rock bottom. I realized I couldn't continue to do life the way I had been doing it. The good news is, Jesus was the rock waiting for me at the bottom. He was my hope when my decisions led to my brokenness. He loved me. He patiently waited for me to come to my senses and choose Him. He didn't judge me. He didn't accuse me of my sins. He lifted me up when I felt ugly, dirty and shamed. That's love – true love. And it's the only reason I can share these stories with you. I'm not bound anymore. I'm free. My heart has been exposed in the most amazing way. The ugly trees that created a lifestyle of sexual sin and unhealthy relationships have been cut down. The love of Jesus lifted me out of the pit and set my feet on a rock (Psalms 40:2).

His love is a light when you're in a deep, dark tunnel. There is no place you could go to be separated from it. His love heals every broken piece of your heart. Like a free gift, all you have to do is accept it. It's not enough to read and hear other people talk about it, you have to receive it for yourself. Recognize the situations in your life where God's love is present and give thanks for it. The love of God is the answer to your brokenness. It is so powerful. It will reach you wherever you are, and will be like a light in every place of your heart. His love will reach you when you feel like you're too far gone and when you feel all alone. If you will open your heart and release the pain that's been stored, you will experience the redemption and restoration that He has for you. This isn't something you can do by yourself and, thanks to the death and resurrection of Jesus, you don't have to. Invite Jesus in and receive His love. A simple prayer is all it takes.

"Jesus, I welcome you into this moment and receive your love. Will you search my heart? Will you reveal the chains that's been preventing me from going all in with you? Amen."

As God begins to reveal issues of your heart, the next step is to allow God to reveal the lies, beliefs and mindsets preventing you from reaching specific milestones and dreams. If you're like me, you want to go all in with the things of God. The things that light up your heart and set your soul on fire. I'm a girl with many dreams, and I believe each of them will be achieved. I'm not afraid to dream, even if it's far-fetched or *out there*. I believe in my dreams and the gifts that God has placed in me. As a mentor, it is my biggest delight when mentees pick up on this same passion. To know that my words encouraged someone to keep going even when they faced opposition; that is my greatest joy. So let this be your reminder to keep going. Your journey may be just starting or maybe you're in year 15, wherever you are, God is with you. His light is leading you. Embrace it. As you walk your journey, stay in God's love.

Sometimes things will get in the way. Shame, guilt, hatred, or other things may come to the surface and your actions will result from these unhealthy issues. Acknowledge it. Release it and don't let it pull you off track on your journey. These things will slow you down or cause you to fall. They are a contrast to God's love, so be aware of them so you can avoid them.

If you fall short or make a mistake, you can always get back up. You can always start again. You can always repent and receive God's grace and mercy. He doesn't hold a record of what you did wrong. He releases you the moment you do it. That's the reason Jesus went to the cross. Don't punish yourself. God doesn't do that. He loves you because He understands, love has the power to change. So take a deep breath and let love lead you to where you're supposed to be.

CHAINS WITHIN YOUR HEART

No matter how fast you run, your chains will always slow you down.

When you spend time dreaming or creating goals, do you ever feel stuck or overwhelmed? Do you ever feel unable to execute your plans, or feel like something is preventing you from moving forward? Imagine waking up and all your biggest dreams and desires were your reality. There are unseen challenges and obstacles preventing that from happening.

For the sake of this chapter, let's call those things chains. Chains are deeply rooted and can be emotional, mental, or spiritual. The purpose of a chain is to restrain or restrict you from full movement. Physical chains will stop you from completing physical activities. Emotional, mental, and spiritual chains affect your beliefs as you complete daily activities and plan for the future. Some may call it baggage. Some may call it bondage. In a Biblical context, you could call it a stronghold. It's like an invisible force that prevents you from moving past a specific point. Anytime you try to get ahead in life, these things show up as obstacles and challenges that you don't know how to overcome.

If you look at a physical chain, you will see that it's a

collection of metal links joined together to form a longer link. Each piece secures the link it is connected with and together they become unbreakable. This is great when it's used to stabilize objects and machinery, but imagine if you had something like this wrapped around your arms where you couldn't be free. Take that same thought and apply it to chains wrapped around your dreams where you couldn't achieve them. What if the location you live in today is the only place you're allowed to live; no opportunity to advance or increase your finances, your business or any aspect of your life. Some people may be okay with that, but you aren't. You believe there's more out there for you. You want to change, grow and develop. You can do that, when you break your chains.

Let's look at spiritual chains. Second Corinthians 10:4 states "The weapons we fight with are not the weapons of the world. On the contrary, they have divine power to demolish strongholds (NIV)." I call them chains, the Bible calls them strongholds. What are strongholds? A collection of mindsets and beliefs that are in conflict with the knowledge of God. God is the spirit of truth. Anything that isn't from Him, is a lie. Therefore, a stronghold is a collection of lies and misguided beliefs linked together and creating issues in multiple areas of your life. It's time to break these things and create patterns that empower and encourage you to achieve your dreams.

Did you know chains can be generational? Have you ever met someone who has a physical illness and others in their family had it too? There is a reason why doctors ask you to identify your family history. Doctors understand some diseases and disorders are hereditary, passed down from generation to generation. Truly, there are a lot of things that are hereditary. Just like diseases and disorders, sometimes we are dealing with issues that affected our parents and grandparents. We are a product of our environment. We repeat actions that we have witnessed from others. If other people in your family went to college, created a business, or had prominent careers, it's going to be instilled in you to do similar things. If people in your family struggled with finances, experienced bad relationships or chronic illness, you may be accustomed to those things. The spiritual, mental and emotional challenges stopping you from achieving your goals are probably stopping your family members. Regardless of your family dynamics, you are in control of your life and you have the power to do things differently. Procrastination, lack of motivation, depression, debt, greed, anger, anxiety, lack of self control – whatever it is, you can be free when you identify these things and replace them with the truth.

Releasing the Chains

Before you can release the chains and experience freedom, you have to identify the problems they're creating in your life. Since chains are sometimes hidden, looking at patterns is a great way to identify them. Write down some of your experiences in life, both good and bad - school, romantic, friendship, or financial experiences. Circle or highlight the issues that keep coming up. In a curious and non judgmental way, ask yourself a few questions. When did these situations start? Why do you keep doing it? How do you feel when you do it? What are some of your thoughts or beliefs around those things? It's okay if you don't know the answer to all of these questions, but the spirit of curiosity may lead to deeper understanding.

A couple years ago, I realized I had a pattern of financial hardship. Every two or three years, I would be over my head in debt. I would get a promotion and create a plan to pay off credit cards and loans. Then after one or two years of doing well, I would find myself in debt again. It started in 2016 when I quit my job randomly and was experiencing so much poverty, I could barely afford toothpaste and toilet paper. I got a really good job working at a warehouse and started working 40-50 hours a week to get out of the hole. I had a roommate, so bills were relatively low, and I had a nice sized savings account. In 2018, things changed. I quit my job again, and started down a path of financial hardship. The savings was gone, I no longer had a roommate, and bills were over my head, again. I didn't know how I kept ending up in situations like that. I felt miserable.

In 2019, I started working a better job and moved in with another roommate. I lowered my expenses, paid off my debt, and developed a good routine adding to my savings account. Guess what happened in 2023? Another season of hardship. Although I didn't quit my job, the same patterns were following me. My roommate was gone and, at this point in my life, I owned my own home. I had enough money to pay all the major bills, but not enough money for food and gas. So I used my credit card like it was extra income. My life was so overwhelming. I was devastated with the way things were going. I was tired of having good years and bad years.

The way I used my credit card was a problem. I couldn't afford the things I was buying, and I gave in to my desires, instead of practicing delayed gratification. When I didn't have money, I used my credit card. It was easy to justify a five dollar cheeseburger, but I was spending five dollars on cheeseburgers, hundreds of dollars on shopping, and thousands of dollars on other random things. I never did it all in one week, but those little things added up. I knew it was bad when I paid off a $7,000 credit card bill and, within 3 years, was faced with another $7,000 balance sitting on my credit card. I had a problem. I needed help. My financial problems were bad. My pain was worse. The problem was what I saw on the outside, the pain was what lingered deep within my heart. I kept trying to fix the problem without healing the pain. The problem kept reoccurring until the pain was resolved.

Pain is like an alarm system for the body. It tells us when intruders are present and when things aren't the way they're supposed to be. Broken bones are painful because pieces of your body aren't functioning the way it was designed. Like a well oiled machine, every body part fits perfectly together, and when things aren't flowing together, it interrupts the natural process. The pain is a wake up call; a reminder to get things checked out.

Problems are meant to be fixed. Pain is meant to be healed. This is true for physical pain as well as emotional pain. Your problems will go away when you heal your pain. Overeating, overspending, sleeping around, getting drunk or high – these are problems but the pain is deeper than that. God wants to heal the pain. He wants to resolve it, and take it away completely. He wants to show you where it came from and how to overcome it. Not only that, but God wants to go through the pain with you. He wants to talk you through it. He wants to be the light guiding you out of the dark and broken places. Your dreams can't live there. It's time to come up and come out of those places. It's time to release. Release the hardship. Release the pain. Release the hurt. Release the shame. All of these things are enforcing the chains.

Whatever happened in the past is in the past. When you hold on to those things, you keep yourself stuck there. It's important to learn how to let go. It may not happen at one time, but you will gradually learn over time. As you do this, you're going to see your biggest and wildest dreams come true. You're going to see and feel a difference within yourself. The areas where you once had low self esteem, you're going to have an increased level of confidence. The areas where you once were insecure, you're going to feel safe and secure because the chains are broken.

Breaking the Chains

The chains you wrestle with are having an internal struggle between the person you are currently and the person you're meant to be. If you want to have a new beginning, what are you willing to let go of to move forward? Imagine God opening a door and allowing you to see into your future, but you can't walk into it because something is holding you back. God is standing in this moment encouraging you to walk forward and enjoy all the things He has for you, but you can't bring those things from the past. The chains won't allow you to experience God's best. They'll let you get close but they won't allow you to be free; they'll always pull you back.

It's time to break those chains. It's time to be completely free. There is greatness on the inside of you, waiting to be unleashed. The chains have held you back long enough but now - today - it's time for a new beginning. This new beginning is everything you've always wanted and everything you've always hoped for. It's an opportunity to do things differently – a do-over, if you will. God is redeeming the time and restoring everything you think you lost. You can start again, and you can have whatever you set your mind to.

The only thing you have to do is make a decision to break every chain. The way to do it can be summed up in one word – surrender. Surrender every negative thought that you have about yourself. Surrender the lies that other people said about you. Surrender the harmful things that others did to you. Just surrender. Lay it down at God's feet. Reveal it all to Him. Tell Him how you were treated and how you felt. Release everything. Lay it down. Let it go.

This may not be an easy task, especially if you've done a good job of holding it all in. But in order to break the chains, you have to let it go. As you do this, I can already tell, you're about to experience your new beginning. The sun is getting ready to break through the darkness in your life. You're getting ready to be completely and totally free. If you want that, this is your moment to receive it. Take a deep breath and let's walk in it!

Journey to Wholeness

WELCOME TO
WHOLENESS

*"If any man be in Christ, he is a new creation: old things are passed away;
behold all things are become new." 2 Corinthians 5:17 KJV*

When a tree rots it decomposes from the inside out.[1] This
is a process often called heart rot. It can take years for the
external part of the tree to look rotten. But when bacteria and
fungi enters it leads to death and decay. The best way to treat
a dying tree is to cut it off.[2] It's very unlikely to restore a tree
that is completely rotten on the inside. The journey to
wholeness is like a transition from a dead tree to a lively tree.
A healing process that isn't available for trees, is available for
you and I. Wholeness is all about transitioning out of things
that are dead and experience things that are alive. God restores
every part of you and makes it new. He has the power to go
deep within our heart and identify the roots that need to be
destroyed, while planting seeds that need to be planted.

Wholeness was the original intent of creation. When God
created the world, He made you complete. Everything was
truly perfect. All of your needs and wants were met because
you were exactly how He wanted you to be. He formed you
with His hands and blew breath in you. Because of His Spirit
living in you, you have everything you need to complete the

assignments He has given to you, but you can't do it in the flesh. It can only be done in the spirit.

This fleshly body, with brown skin, tan skin, light skin, or dark skin is the least important thing we have. The most important thing is our spirit. God created you as a spirit first, then he gave you a soul and placed you in a body. The soul is composed of your mind, will and emotions. If you think of the body in layers, the starting point is the spirit - that's the core of who you are. The next layer is the soul. The final layer is the body - that's what everyone sees. God told the prophet Samuel in First Samuel 16, that man looks at the outer appearance, but God looks at the heart. This is the importance of having a relationship with God; every part of you becomes connected. The spirit speaks and the soul responds and then the body.

God is a gentle God. He has given you free will. He will not force you to connect with Him, but throughout your journey, you will learn that this is the best way to be successful. This is the best way to achieve your dreams and overcome challenges and obstacles that consistently weigh you down. Connection with God is the way to eternal life in heaven and abundant life here on earth. You were designed for this, but because of life and the sin nature within the world, there are many things pulling you into disconnection. You may not be able to see it, but you can feel it. You can feel when things are off and when you're not approaching situations the way you normally would. You feel down and out. You feel drained. Instead of waking up at 6 am, and getting ready for your work day, you roll out of bed at 7:30 and barely make it to work on time. You stop caring for yourself the way you used to. Something changed and you don't know what it is.

Have you been feeling distant from God? Have you ever had thoughts that you were too far gone – you've made too many mistakes or sinned too many times? If so, I want you to know that is a lie. Jesus died so you can have restoration. Jesus wants to bring you back to your original purpose. The purpose outlined in Genesis 1:28; Be fruitful and multiply. Subdue and have dominion over the earth. Jesus died on the cross because He loves you. The moment you accept His love, you will be restored. Then it's important to give love to yourself and release the penalty you've required yourself to pay. Jesus paid it all. There is no shame, judgement or condemnation that can take that away. Accept His love and begin to walk in the spirit.

As you look in the mirror and reflect on your life, do you see yourself as whole and thriving in every area? If not, what areas do you feel like you're missing something? Have you fully given yourself love to those areas? For example, if you are struggling in the area of romantic relationships, and waiting for a faith-filled marriage, have you allowed love to enter those places?

Love can fulfill your romantic desires. Look at the scripture – First Corinthians 13:4 says "love is patient, love is kind. It does not envy, it does not boast, it is not proud." Now apply this to marriage. Start saying things like "I will be patient in my singleness. I will be kind to myself as I wait for my spouse. I will not be jealous of others who are in a healthy relationship or marriage. I will be humble as I wait for my spouse. This is how you apply love to this area of your life. These are biblical truths that you can stand on and hopefully they give you strength for your journey. You don't know how long your singleness journey will be, but as you wait, do it with patience, kindness, humbleness, and celebration of others. Don't become impatient, mean and jealous with your process. I understand, this is easier said than done, but continue to sit with God and bring these things to Him whenever they appear.

You can apply this method to any situation that you are struggling with and use God's love to overcome. This is a principle that is rooted in patience, kindness, celebration of others, humility, forgiveness, calm and peacefulness, honesty, protection, trust, hopefulness and perseverance. I have studied the passage of First Corinthians 13:4-7 in great detail and I've applied this principle of love to multiple areas of my life. Before I could change any of my actions, I allowed God's love to fill that area of my heart. From financial hardship and raising a family to mental health and praying for physical healing - God can handle all of it. He can make all things new.

He starts with your mind and your beliefs. Take time, right now, to identify the areas that you're struggling with and allow God's love to fill you up. Fully surrender those things and write scriptures that align with where you want to be. As you write these things, believe them with your heart. Believe that it will change your life. Believe that it will make you new. It may not happen overnight, but this is the starting point.

Wholeness Requires Faith

When I think about wholeness, I think of a story in the Bible of a woman who struggled with an illness for 12 years. If you read in Luke 8, you see that her illness caused her to bleed. The doctors didn't have an answer for her and there was no cure. She was considered unclean and everything she touched was unclean. She was probably lonely. Maybe she didn't have a lot of friends and didn't go to many places. Imagine how hard this may have been. This woman was watching life happen around her. For 12 years, she dreamed and believed for change, and never received it. But she didn't give up. One day she heard that Jesus was coming to town and she wanted him to heal her. Despite Jewish law, she went to his location, and she pressed through the crowds to get to him. She was desperate to reach him and was willing to do something wild and courageous.

Due to the large numbers of people, she had to stretch, and reach out for him, but all she could touch was the hem of his garment, which is the edge or the bottom of a piece of clothing. This means she was close to the ground. Maybe she was pushed, maybe she fell, maybe she was crawling, and getting stepped on - but she kept going. She was willing to get dirty for her wholeness. It was worth that much to her. How much is it worth to you? If you could be completely free from the pain you've been feeling, and never deal with it again, what would you do? Sometimes you have to fight through crowds, fight through societal norms and do what no one else has ever done in order to receive what you want.

This woman heard about a man who heals people and she believed He could help her. So she put forth actions to experience the change she wanted to see. Despite the challenges and opposition, she pressed through the crowds to reach him and her life was changed with one touch. The Bible says instantly the blood dried up and she was healed. Can I tell you a secret? The piece of clothing that the woman touched didn't have power - it was her faith. Her faith created actions, which created change. Her mind was made up and she believed healing was possible for her. The moment she changed her belief, she was healed. Your mindsets and beliefs show up in your actions. It doesn't matter what your physical situation looks like when you have a mindset to trust and believe God. This woman received healing because she believed it was possible for her. She fought for it. She worked for it.

"Daughter, your faith has healed you. Go in peace." Luke 8:48 NIV

This is what Jesus said to the woman after she touched him. This is one of my favorite stories in the Bible. I grew up hearing about this story in church but when I read it for myself, I felt like I could relate to the woman. I had been there - going through seasons where I was alone, fighting battles of sexual addictions, depression, low self esteem and other things. Just like the woman, I heard about the power of Jesus, but I didn't experience change until I reached out for Him.

I didn't meet Jesus on a dirt road. I met him in my bedroom as a teenager desperately in need of change. I also met Him in my apartment, as a young adult, experiencing another broken heart from another broken relationship. Likewise, I met Him on the floor of my office, as a working professional, crying out to The One who could rescue me from the intrusive thoughts within my mind. I've met Jesus multiple times and each encounter is exactly what I needed to experience a new beginning, a new start, or a new direction with my life. Jesus doesn't show up only in grandiose moments where you're breaking and hurting on the inside, He shows up daily.

Anytime you call His name – reach out to Him – and believe, He hears you. Your faith activates your relationship with Him. Just like the woman with the issue of blood had faith to receive healing from Jesus, you must have faith to receive answers to your prayers.

Wholeness within Your Beliefs

What do you believe about you? Since faith is the requirement for prayers to be answered, sometimes you have to reflect on your beliefs. Do you believe you can have whatever you declare? If so, what things are you speaking and declaring over your life? The Bible says life and death are in the power of the tongue. Your words have power. When you speak things over yourself it leads to fruitfulness. Believing is the challenging part, especially when you are believing for something big and, currently, you don't see it. Believe anyways.

"Do not conform to the pattern of this world, but be transformed by the renewing of your mind. Then you will be able to test and approve what God's will is – his good, pleasing and perfect will." Romans 12:2 NIV

The Bible says you will be transformed when you renew your mind. Words of affirmation are a great way to renew your mind. Repeat words, phrases and scriptures that align with your spirit. The word renew means to resume after an interruption, return to, or come back to. The goal is to come back to your original form, the authentic version of you - the version of you that God always wanted you to be. That requires you to see yourself achieving everything you always wanted to achieve and believe it's possible for you. Envision the life you always wanted. What does it look like? What does it sound like and feel like? Now is the time to believe those things can happen, even if they're far away, if you can see it within your imagination, you can see it realistically. All great inventions start somewhere. Imagine the life you want to live, get connected to it, and start implementing things daily to make it your reality.

THE JOURNEY TO CONNECTION

"The thief comes to steal, kill, and destroy. I came that you might have life and have it abundantly." John 10:10 KJV

Imagine connecting your phone to a charger before bed and waking up to realize it's dead because the charger wasn't plugged into the wall. Has that ever happened to you? It's definitely not a great start to the day, but let's talk about that for a second. Why didn't the charger work? Although it was connected to the phone, there was no power. The power comes from the electricity within the wall socket. The charger is useless by itself.

Using this same analogy, let's imagine the phone is you. You are accomplishing the calling on your life and sometimes your battery is drained - drained from all the meetings you've been to, all the arguments and disagreements you've dealt with, and hardships with work and school. How do you recharge after a busy week? Is it church or spending time with friends? Maybe you feel recharged after attending a small group or doing something fun. Is that enough?

Is it possible to be plugged into all of these positive groups and still feel drained? Or maybe you're plugged into things that used to charge and energize you but now, it doesn't. Instead of feeling full and satisfied after church, you feel overwhelmed and tired. Small groups aren't the same and your friends gossip and overload you with all their drama. If this is the way you've been feeling, it's time to check the power source. Your friends don't have the power to recharge you all by themselves. They need God, just like you need God. Friendships are fulfilling when both of you are connected to God first, then each other. A church gathering is just a gathering, if God's Spirit isn't present. The power comes from His Spirit and His Spirit lives in you.

Are you going through the motions with God, trying to do the right things while feeling disconnected? Do you pray, read your Bible, and go to church expecting your life to change, but continue to feel like something is missing? That's a key indicator that you're disconnected.

When the feeling of disconnection is present, you will not be content unless you address the issue within your heart. Let's be clear. You can be fully invested in church, friendships and business and still feel disconnected. Think of connection as alignment. When your car isn't aligned, it still works, but it operates better when there is an alignment. I know that's a bad analogy, but, hopefully, you get the point. When you're connected, your beliefs, thoughts and actions are on one accord.

You can enjoy daily activities with a mind set on God, and God's Spirit will give you divine insights that allow you to be productive. Your daily life may be simple – school, work, home – but your relationship with God doesn't have to be. God can take the small things and make them big things. It's a mindset shift. You may not feel any different when He does it, but internally you'll know something is different. You may experience a change within your confidence level. You may experience a change within your attitude and the way you approach challenges. As you take control of your mind and prioritize listening to God, you'll see things change within your life. These are real, heart to heart moments that you can enjoy with God all throughout the day. This is connection.

Connection Comes Through Time Spent with God

There is a God-sized hole within you that only God can fill. As the creator of the universe, and your creator, God designed you with purpose and life doesn't feel the same when it's missing. Like a phone that needs to be connected to power when the battery is low, so do you. If you're struggling in any area of your life, that is an area that God wants to connect with you. You have to give Him access to that part of your heart.

One day while reading my Bible, I wrote the scripture John 10:10 and then, I had a conversation with God in my journal.

Where is this abundant life you speak of? I'm single and dreaming of the man that's perfect for me, but I don't see him coming any time soon. I'm living in poverty, working a job that I hate, and I'm trying to tell people about wholeness. Right now, that abundant life looks like a pipe dream, something I wish I had. With all due respect, where are you, God? Where is my new beginning? Why does it seem like it's so far away? Why does it seem like I'm wishing on a star with no plan and no direction on how to achieve my dreams? Does wholeness only apply to broken hearts due to relationships, or can you give wholeness for this broken heart due to life?

This was a rough season. I felt horrible every day I went to work. I was connected with God on Sundays while attending church and disconnected Monday through Friday. I didn't understand my purpose at that job. I thought about leaving and going to a different company. I thought I would be happier in another position that paid more money, but every time I applied and interviewed for a new job, I didn't have peace. God was building something on the inside of me that required me to stay and press into Him.

New Beginnings is not about running away from internal pain – it's about addressing it. You can change your address and go to a new place, but the same attitudes and mindsets will follow you. It takes more than a drive or a flight to get rid of those things. To be free from my toxic mindsets, attitudes and beliefs required work.

Things began to change when I began to chase after God. Initially, I had a poor work ethic. I arrived late and didn't do my best work. One day, I started inviting God into the office with me. I made the decision to be obedient and I learned to connect with Him daily. Through music, journaling, deep breathing and intentional quiet times, I spent time with Him. I learned how to pray without ceasing. I imitated the actions of the woman with the issue of blood and I utilized my faith to experience God's supernatural breakthrough. He didn't change my situation automatically, but He changed my mindset instantly. Like Romans 12:2, I was being transformed by the renewing of my mind, and that allowed me to understand God's will for my life.

As I did this, God gave me ideas and strategies that led to success within the workplace. I believe other people saw the improvement within my work and the changes that were taking place within my heart. Ultimately, being connected to God led to two promotions within one year and a $15,000 raise that I never imagined. I began to see God's goodness overflow in my life. I experienced overflow with my finances, my dreams being achieved, and ministry. To this day, I am accomplishing the purpose that God created me for because I stay connected to His Spirit. I listen when He speaks. I consult with Him prior to making decisions. I don't want anything to get me off track and I know the enemy will use anything to slow me down and stop me from walking in the fire that God has given me. When I'm disconnected from God, I use worldly things to deal with my issues. In high school and college, I used relationships. As an older adult, I have used alcohol, tobacco, sexual sin, and depression. I choose to live a life connected to God because I refuse to let the enemy win.

God has a purpose and a plan for you. He has plans to prosper you and not to harm you (Jeremiah 29:11). He wants you to succeed and thrive. And God knows how to make it happen. What areas in your life are overflowing? What areas in your life do you want to overflow? The answer to these questions can be love, joy, finances, friendships – anything.

This is what you can expect from the Lord, but it is only available through connection. Make a decision right now that you don't want to be disconnected. Today is the day you experience abundance in all areas. It is as simple as asking for it and believing that you can have it. Pray this prayer over yourself as you prepare for the next chapter.

Prayer: Dear God, I invite you in this space as I read and receive what you have for me. Open my heart and speak to me. Lead me into a place of abundance. As I reflect on my life, reveal the area where I am experiencing lack. I give this portion to you and patiently wait for you to fill me up. In Jesus' name, Amen!

GETTING CONNECTED
TO YOUR SPIRIT

"And I will pray the Father, and he shall give you another Comforter, that he may abide with you forever; even the Spirit of truth; whom the world cannot receive, because it seeth him not, neither knoweth him: but ye know him: for he dwelleth with you, and shall be in you." John 14: 16-17 KJV

Let's get connected. I don't want you to read this book and leave an opportunity on the table to practice what you're learning. I want you to get connected to God in such a way where you feel His presence with you and hear His voice speaking to you. Like the scripture says, God's Holy Spirit lives in you. When He speaks you can hear Him, if you've been taught to listen to His voice.

I like to slow down, bring my thoughts in and talk out loud. That's how I communicate with God. When I talk, it is as if He were sitting or standing right beside me. I can feel His presence and I know He is with me. He speaks to me and leads me to the answers of questions that I've been asking. That's what I mean when I say connection – our spirit aligns with God's spirit. As a Christian and a believer, this is a biblical truth. Jesus talks about it often as He was preparing for the cross. In John 14:26-27, He says the Father will send the Comforter and He will teach you all things and bring things back to your remembrance. Have you ever looked for something and didn't know where it was? This happens to me all the time. I walk into a room looking for something important and say out loud: God, where did I put that item? Then I'm reminded of the location and find exactly what I'm looking for. I believe the Holy Spirit shows up in small moments like that, as well as big moments where He tells me not to say or do something I really want to do.

The majority of your dreams and desires come from a seed planted by God. Some of them come from impure seeds planted by jealousy, hatred, and other forms of wickedness, but not all of them. When you get connected to your spirit, God will teach you how to understand the deepest parts of you, where your desires come from, and the reason behind those things. Anytime you're struggling with things like finances, hardship at your job, pressure from friends or family, or pain from past trauma, connection will lead to spiritual insight and God-given strategies that allow you to overcome those challenges. The best way to get connected to God's spirit is to connect with your spirit. Your spirit was designed to be one with God, but you have to welcome His presence and invite Him into your heart. Imagine that your spirit is a house. You are the owner of this house and you have permission of who you allow in. God is not going to force you to let him in. The Bible says in Revelations 3:20 that He stands at the door and knocks. It's time to let Him in.

For the person that's never done this, I want to break it all the way down so that it makes sense and you understand it's not a foreign process. At the same time, I want to express that everyone is different. The response one person receives through connection, may not be the response you receive. Try it this way, and if it doesn't work, try it another way. Whatever you do, keep aiming and striving for connection.

Physically, what happens when you get connected to your spirit?

When you get connected to your spirit, your breathing will slow down and the ability to focus will increase. Sometimes you can feel a shift within your mind or within the atmosphere around you. You may feel things on your skin, like goosebumps or cold chills. Hopefully, you will feel calm and at peace - that is the goal anyways. If you struggle with Attention-Deficit/Hyperactivity Disorder, ADHD, this is a tool that could allow you to be successful in daily activities without the use of medicine – or limited amounts of medicine. Mental Health professionals would call this practicing mindfulness. There are plenty of studies that show the benefit of implementing things like this in your daily life. Getting connected to your spirit can lead to clarity with work or specific assignments, allowing you to be more productive.

Take a moment to slow down, get to a quiet place around you, and take deep breaths from your diaphragm. Breathe in for 8 counts and breathe out for 8 counts. Just breathe. Notice any thoughts that may appear, push them aside, and just focus on your breath.

Mentally, what happens when you get connected to your spirit?

Quiet Thoughts. You will have the ability to quiet your thoughts. In a room full of noise and chaos, you can quiet the noise and be still while the world around you continues to turn. Our thoughts can be loud as an ocean sometimes. We have noise from our family, friends and complete strangers on social media. It is easy to have overwhelming thoughts, but it is our job to silence them. They may be loud when you first start doing things like this, but they will slow down as you continue to practice.

Once that happens, you can experience the peaceful quietness that arrives as you overcome intrusive thoughts. Intrusive thoughts are thoughts that appear randomly. They are invasive, unkind, and usually not encouraging you to do anything God is telling you to do. They distract and complicate your ability to focus, think or hear clearly. They come as an attack from the enemy. Intrusive thoughts are demonic and it's your responsibility to wage war against them.

Deeper Understanding. Words, ideas and desires will be identified when you are connected to your spirit. You will hear or be reminded of things that you weren't initially thinking about. These thoughts will come out of nowhere, but they'll be different than intrusive thoughts. They'll be kind, loving and full of God's word. You will have an understanding deeper than your conscious mind can reveal. Your conscious mind only holds so much information; your subconscious mind is like a deep well of knowledge. Dreams and desires you had as a child may still be in you. You thought you forgot about it or gave up on it, but it was stored within your subconscious mind. As you get connected to your spirit, God may reveal passions and talents that He wants you to pursue. That is the power of The Spirit speaking and bringing things to the forefront of your mind. You will see, hear and understand things clearly.

Mindset Shift. This process creates a shift within your mindset. You may not realize this, but you are fighting battles in your mind that Jesus Christ can give you the victory over. You have inventions and business ideas greater than Steve Jobs that would radically change your life and impact others, but you're stuck inside a mind that's overwhelmed; a mind that second guesses everything, judges and criticizes constantly. If your mind is full of hatred, envy and evil thoughts because life isn't going as expected, it's time to be free. Freedom is available to you as you take the necessary steps to renew your mind and break those chains.

Take another moment to slow down and practice breathing from your diaphragm. If it helps, set a timer for five or 10 minutes and turn everything off for those minutes. Make this an intentional time to get connected. Identify the words, thoughts and images that may appear. If necessary, write them down on a piece of paper. Just breathe and listen. Once the timer is up, pray and ask God to reveal the meaning of anything you saw or heard.

I'm telling you, this works. I lived in a broken mental state for far too long and, through practices like these, I realized I have the power to change. If you implement the things I'm sharing with you, you can live the life you want to live. You can dream big dreams and achieve them. The goals that you have for business, work, friendships and family can be achieved when you connect with God. Like I mentioned before, connection is all about spending time and communicating. It's not hard. Try it today. Be intentional to set time for connection with God. Give yourself 30 minutes or an hour and stay the whole time. You may not feel any different after five minutes. You may not feel different after one day, but if you continue to show up with God, He will continue to show up with you. You are creating a space for your spirit to open up and release anything it's been holding on to. Your spirit may be holding on to things from five, 10 or 15 years ago. It's time to release. Be gentle and kind to yourself. Your spirit needs to feel safe. You can create safety when you speak, listen, and understand your spirit.

Speak to Your Spirit

Say these words. "Dear heart, I see you. I hear you. I'm right here with you."

When you speak to your spirit, it listens. I know people that like to place their hand on their body as a physical representation of touching their spirit. I've seen people put their hand on their belly, on their chest, or on their forehead as they speak. Whatever makes it easy for you – that's what you should do.

Speaking out loud is another option. I won't say it's required, but I will share this with you. Everything you hear is typically audible, right? When you watch tv or talk to other people, the sounds are projected in the air and you hear it audibly. Speaking to your spirit should have the same effect. Your physical ears need to hear what you're saying. Thinking these words will not produce the same effect. Say it out loud.

This is something I do daily and it truly provides a moment

of release. When I have quiet time with God, I speak my prayers out loud. I cry and release my pain out loud. Saying things out loud creates reinforcement. It's not weird. It's not strange. It is a form of intimacy and you deserve to give that to yourself.

Listen to Your Spirit

Have you ever heard someone say they had a gut instinct or a feeling on the inside of them and they knew something bad was about to happen? That was their spirit speaking to them. Some theologians refer to a person's spirit as intuition and some refer to it as a person's second brain. I think it comes down to the conscious mind versus the subconscious mind.

Regardless of how you view your spirit, I want you to understand, it speaks. It has a voice. The more you connect with it, the louder the voice will be, and you will recognize it. For someone just starting out, listen or acknowledge the words you hear while in quiet time. Use a journal, write the date, speak to your spirit and write down the words, phrases, or thoughts that appear. Then take time to decipher it and ask yourself – is this God speaking, the enemy speaking, or intrusive thoughts speaking? Just a reminder: God speaking will always be aligned with the Word of God.

Let's try it again. Say this out loud. "Dear heart, I see you. I hear you. I'm right here with you. This is a safe space to open up and release. I'm listening."

Understand Your Spirit

Have you ever tried to have a conversation with someone who didn't speak the same language as you? If so, you know how challenging it is to share a message with them. The more you try to communicate, the less they understand. Some people start using their hands or pointing to specific things to try to relay a message. When I was in Spain for the first time, I went to my hotel and realized I didn't have a European adapter for my charger. I couldn't charge my phone. So I went to the closest store and asked a lady to help me, but she didn't speak any English. After 10 minutes of failed communications, I pulled out my physical charger, pointed at my cell phone and pointed to the adapter; then, she finally understood what I was saying and led me in the right direction. I learned that without proper communication you cannot have a proper connection. It is imperative that you understand what your spirit is saying and feeling. That is the only way to have a good connection.

While listening to your spirit, you may hear specific words that resonate with you. You may hear things from your childhood or family experiences. Allow yourself to listen, be curious, ask deeper questions and uncover the meaning. Just like in a dream, images and flashbacks have a purpose and if your spirit is revealing things like this to you, it's for a reason. Stay in the moment as long as you need, to make sure you understand it. Don't rush it because the longer you stay there, the more your spirit will reveal.

When I first started learning about connection, I didn't know if it was God speaking or my own thoughts, but over time, I learned the difference. This spirit-filled voice led me into God's arms in 2018 when I was at my lowest and most painful place. The voice said, "You're strong enough to get through this." I had never heard God speak so clearly and His words were very direct.

COMMUNITY AND CONNECTION

Proper connection with God and your spirit leads to collaboration, conversation and community among others. According to Merriam-Webster, collaboration is the act of two or more people working together to produce or create something. Conversation is a talk, between two or more people, in which news and ideas are exchanged. And community is a group of people living in the same place or having a particular characteristic in common. Another definition said it is a feeling of fellowship with others – I really like that one. Regardless of how you describe these three words, take a moment to reflect and ask yourself how do they play out in your life. This chapter goes back to the description of a cell phone being plugged in and charged. When you are surrounded by the right people, they have the power to enlighten and enrich your life. At the same time, the wrong people have the power to drain you and pull you away from things that matter to you.

Community is more than a group of people coming together in the same place, but its about working and building together. This is only possible when you find the people that you trust and you can be yourself. Think of a memory when you were around fun, loving and supportive people. You were smiling, laughing and having a good time. Maybe you were at your favorite restaurant, enjoying your favorite meal or simply engaging with your favorite person. As you think back on those memories, I'm sure you can still feel the positivity and excitement from that day. That's a result of connection. Although you can't go back in time and relive those moments, you can go back in your mind and remember the emotions. You can remember the smells, hear the sounds, and feel the feelings. This is one of my favorite things to do, not only with memories, but also with things I imagine and anticipate for the future. You can achieve whatever you want to achieve in life. When you're clear on what you want, God will allow you to connect with the right people at the right time to make it happen. The visions and dreams living on the inside of you are for an appointed time. All you have to do is believe in them.

When I was fresh out of college, I longed for the day where I owned a house. In 2019, I lived in an old run-down condo with my sister. This condo was horrible, the ceiling was falling down, and sometimes the lock on the front door got jammed where I couldn't get in. That old, rugged condo had a back door and a small field of grass. I used to stand in the back, look out in the field, and dream about the day when I purchased my first home. I spent hours imagining and dreaming about a home. I did this so often, I knew what it would feel like, look like, and sound like. Two years later, that dream became a reality. Now, I can walk outside onto my back porch, sit on the deck, and enjoy my backyard – just like I did with the condo. Talk about a dream come true. Even though I didn't have it in 2019, I believed for it. Because I believed for it, I worked for it. I talked about it. I knew it was going to happen. When you believe for something strong enough, you will achieve it. The spirit inside of you will connect you to the right people, places, and opportunities. All you have to do is believe. Believing is a form of connection, especially if you have a creative imagination. When you imagine it, you allow yourself to create details within your mind. I believe God is present in those moments when you dream and imagine things that He has placed in your heart.

As others see your heart, dreams, desires, and your light they will choose to align and connect with you. Sometimes they won't understand why they're so drawn to you, but they'll know that you have something different than others. That's your spirit. When someone is connected to their spirit, they can feel, sense, and understand someone else's spirit. That's why it's important to express yourself. Your kindness, your goofiness, your wisdom, and all the other aspects of your personality should be fully expressed anytime you're having conversations.

When community and connection is your goal, you don't have to hide any part of who you are. Your friends won't either. Express yourself in an authentic and transparent format. When doing so, your friends will surround you with love and support anytime you need it. They'll celebrate with you in your biggest wins and mourn with you in your lowest lows. Don't worry about judgement or rejection. Be you. When the community is built on love, support, and respect, that's the perfect foundation for connection. Sometimes you have to evaluate your circle of friends and ask yourself: "What is this community built on and am I showing up authentically within each conversation?"

I remember being connected to a really fun workout group while processing through my breakup and pursuing healing. God was working on my heart, and I decided to work on my health. There were three of us and sometimes others would join in. We met at the local park and our trainer, Coach Tim, gave us workout routines. We ran stadiums, we ran around the track, we also met at a fitness gym to work out using equipment. We were a small community, and it helped me get through a really rough time. My friends would text me to encourage me – it may have seemed random, but it was always exactly when I needed it. We worked out three or four days a week and had a lot of fun doing it. Friendships were formed. Love was given and received. We worked together to achieve weight loss goals. That's it. That was the whole purpose of our time together. It was everything that I needed because it allowed me to get out of my head. Instead of isolating my home, I surrounded myself with friends. That's connection and that is the purpose of community.

God wants us to achieve our dreams. God placed those dreams on the inside of us and He wants to help us fulfill them. Sometimes he hand picks us for a specific location and place to be a part of a team of like-minded individuals. Your dreams will be achieved on the other side of connection. Don't try to do them by yourself. You were never meant to work like that. Some ideas and business plans are too big to carry by yourself. Find a community where you fit in and thrive.

LOVE AND CONNECTION

One day while flying to a writers retreat, I watched a movie about two friends with different personalities. I was 50,000 feet in the air, feeling inspired by a movie that I have seen multiple times. Although they were polar opposites, the friends formed a relationship through love and connection. The girl was like fire and the guy was like ice. He was emotional and unapologetically connected to his feelings; the girl, however, was not. She didn't talk about her feelings because it was uncomfortable for her, but every time they were together, he pulled it out of her. He created a space so safe and relaxed that she could let her guard down and be herself. All throughout the movie she shared her heart with him – her real, true and loving heart – and each time it caught her by surprise. She wasn't used to that. Her family didn't talk about feelings and emotions. They were fireballs. They expressed anger and that was the only emotion they expressed.

Any time she opened up and told him how she felt, he listened and gave her compassion. "I'm sorry you feel that way," he would say, or, "You must be carrying so much." He was emotionally intelligent and led her into safe conversations where she could be seen, heard, and understood. That's all she really wanted. She was creative and passionate about art, but she didn't allow herself to pursue it. You see, she was next in line to run the family business and her dad was counting on her. She didn't want to do it, but even more than that, she didn't want to let him down. So she suppressed her desires and pushed away her true feelings in an attempt to please her family. But those suppressed feelings and desires became explosive. Literally. She would yell, lash out, and scream at people whenever she got overwhelmed. "Maybe your anger is trying to tell you something," her friend told her. She didn't know this, but her unresolved feelings were driving her aggressive behaviors.

This is true for a lot of people and they don't realize it. This is how I lived my childhood. In middle school, I was mean and had a really bad attitude. I lashed out and dealt with a lot of aggressive behavior toward my family and my friends. Everyone knows that teenagers experience changes with their bodies, but how many people take the time to listen to teenagers' thoughts and beliefs about themselves? Not judge or correct them, but just listen. Sometimes people don't need your advice or expertise, they just want you to listen.

I felt ugly when I was in high school. I wanted to fit in with my friends and do whatever the popular kids were doing. I clicked with the "make up girls." Every day we went to school and put on make-up in first period - thick eyeliner, clumpy mascara, foundation, bronzer and blush. We went overboard, but that was the style. Make-up became a really good coverup for the pain of rejection I felt on the inside. I felt like I wasn't enough. I was shy in public, so I didn't talk much, but even when I did, I felt like I couldn't let them see my personality. I wasn't genuine. I thought they were going to reject my eclectic thought processes or my random comments. The world didn't feel safe, so I stayed silent.

Even with my silence, I wanted people to hear me. I wanted to feel safe and supported. I wanted compassion. But I didn't receive that and I didn't know how to give it to myself. Safe spaces are all about listening and not responding, or responding with compassion.

"I see you. I'm here with you. You're not alone. It's going to be okay. Thank you for sharing your heart." This is compassion. This is what it sounds like to allow someone to speak and listening to understand what they're really trying to say. To listen to someone's heart is one of the best things you can do to connect with them.

How amazing is it for someone to see the real, raw and ugly parts within you and still tell you they love you and they're here for you. Most people are afraid of deep connections like this because they don't trust others. They've been abused, rejected, and disrespected too many times. They're trying to protect themselves and protect their peace, so they built walls and won't let anyone have access to them. I get it. I was in the same place, but I decided that I wasn't going to allow my past to hold me down. I chose to release every toxic and broken thing that was ever said and done to me, and I learned to embrace true community and friendship. While doing so, I found true friends that really care. I found friends that listen when I share my heart and respond respectfully when we have conflict. Friendships aren't perfect and conflict is bound to happen, but love allows us to resolve the issue and maintain connection. My friends love me enough to tell me when I hurt their feelings and vice versa. We listen and we don't judge.

You can choose to release the painful memories of your past and embrace open and honest friendships too. If necessary, you may want to start small and work your way up to deep connection. We were made for connection, with God and each other. It's important to let people in. Before you say you can't trust someone, identify if they're trustworthy. Share one thing about yourself, and listen to their response. If you feel loved, supported, and celebrated after that conversation, consider sharing more. You get to decide how much involvement someone has in your life. It's your life and I encourage you to live it with community.

Thinking back to the movie, the girl was afraid of connection, afraid to learn the truth about how she felt, and even more afraid to reveal it with others. Because of this, she couldn't love herself. She couldn't love her dreams, and she couldn't love her friend. She didn't know how. This is true for many people. Love is a word that is thrown around superficially. People say it and they don't mean it. Love should be something we see with actions. Love should be seen through actions like honesty, open communication, forgiveness and grace. Those are examples of things you can give to the ones you love.

Tell the truth when you're speaking with someone. Don't lie to cover up your mistakes. Don't tell half truths. Be completely honest. Talk and communicate openly about things. Forgive and extend grace to others when they hurt you. Let it go. This is an example of love. And sometimes giving these things to others is hard. Sometimes it's a sacrifice to love someone like this. But I can show you multiple examples in the Bible where Jesus loved others like this. Jesus was honest. He didn't lie when talking to the disciples. He wasn't holding secrets and covering things up hoping others wouldn't find out. There were times when He used self-control and He told people not to say anything, but it wasn't from a place of dishonesty or malicious intent. Jesus loved people. You can tell from the way He talked to them.

"Love is patient, love is kind. It does not envy, it does not boast, it is not proud. It does not dishonor others, it is not self-seeking, it is not easily angered, it keeps no record of wrongs. Love does not delight in evil but rejoices with the truth. It always protects, always trusts, always hopes, always perseveres. Love never fails. But where there are prophecies, they will cease; where there are tongues, they will be stilled; where there is knowledge, it will pass away." 1 Corinthians 13:4-8 KJV

Do you fully understand the meaning of love? Are you patient, kind and forgiving, or do you speak negatively and remind yourself of your mistakes? It's important to love you before you try to love others. Whatever is on the inside of you will come out of you.

At the end of the movie the girl reached a breaking point and she was honest with her father. She told him that she didn't want to run the family business; instead, she wanted to pursue art and travel with her friend. For the first time, she shared her heart with her father. There was no anger or aggression, only the true emotions of her broken heart. "I'm sorry, Dad. I'm a bad daughter," she said while kneeling on the ground and crying, "but I don't want to run the family business." The more she talked, the more her dad listened. She continued to reveal that she loved her friend and didn't want to lose him. Her dad wasn't mad at her. He was proud of her. He told her she could never be a bad daughter because he loved her too much. It was a special moment between the two of them. This moment of truth didn't ruin their relationship. It strengthened it. He continued to love her as he let her go to pursue her dreams.

Sometimes we're going to reach a breaking point in life and we will need to be reminded that our Heavenly Father loves us. Our Father will listen to our deepest cry and forgive us our ugliest sins because He loves us. He has always loved us. True connection, with God, or with others, requires love, and love leads to forgiveness, honesty, empathy, compassion, gentleness, and more. It's not forced or fake; it's an authentic response. When you're connected, you can't help but give these things.

People want to be heard and usually when a person lashes out, yells or fusses about a situation, they feel unheard, misunderstood, or mistreated. The longer you walk on your journey, the easier it will be to resolve conflict as they arise. It can be hard to face conflict head on, but the alternative is disconnection and that is worse. Conflict is a natural part of friendship and community. We're humans, we're going to disagree about things. It could be different viewpoints and beliefs, or errors and wrongdoing. The goal shouldn't be to never argue. The goal should be to maintain love and respect regardless of the situation. This is where we apply gentleness, grace and forgiveness. The beauty of love is that there is always an opportunity to make things right.

Connection is a journey. It doesn't happen overnight. It takes time. Similar to mastering a new skill or perfecting a recipe, sometimes you have to try it over and over until you get it right. The ones that truly become masters at something are willing to practice for years, while trusting that it's getting better day by day. Take your time with yourself. Don't rush and don't give up. You deserve to live a life that is fully connected to God, others, and yourself. You can be full everyday as you take care of your spirit, soul, and body. Keep going toward your destination, and embrace wherever you are on your journey.

The Journey of Metamorphosis

A BUTTERFLY IN FLIGHT

Before you were born, your dad and mom had an encounter and your mom became pregnant. This seed, in its early stage, had purpose and destiny from God. You were predestined for greatness. Unfortunately, due to the sin and darkness within this world, you lived your life desperately in need of one thing – salvation and relationship with Jesus. Before you experienced salvation, you lived a normal life, working, eating, and going through the motions, but something was missing. Then you reached a breaking point and you began your new journey with hopes and aspirations of transformation from the Lord. This is what new beginnings looks like. This can be true for anything related to life, happiness, healing, and wholeness. Some people are addicted to drugs and alcohol, while others are addicted to eating and purging. Whatever your struggle is, you can be free from it when you run after the Father and refuse to accept anything other than Him. You can be radically transformed and changed into something unrecognizable. I've seen this to be true in my life and I've seen it to be true in the life of a butterfly.

Have you ever researched the transition process when a caterpillar becomes a butterfly? It's a journey called metamorphosis. There are four separate stages – egg, larva, pupa, and adult.[1] An adult butterfly lays an egg; the egg hatches and becomes a caterpillar. This is the larva stage. While in this stage, the caterpillar eats and grows until it reaches its full potential. When its potential as a caterpillar is reached, it transitions into the pupa stage and forms a chrysalis, where the transformation happens. If you ask a science teacher or biology professor, they can give you a thorough explanation of what happens inside the cocoon, as the caterpillar undergoes this process. The final stage is known as the adult stage and the butterfly emerges.[2] A beautiful insect with colors and unique design is presented, only after it has been through the process.

How cool is that?! Things like this make me fall in love with God and nature all over again. When butterflies develop their wings and transition into a new form, they fly. They don't question if they should remain stable or remain in the same position. They fly. It's designed by nature for them to know how this process works. They don't have to figure it out. They trust the natural flow of nature.

Now is your time to take flight. Transition out of the old things you've been in and embrace the new that is waiting for you. Maybe it's time for something new physically, like a new job or a new car. That is always a good feeling and usually brings a lot of excitement, but even if nothing changes and you're still faced with the same situations, you have the power to embrace a new attitude, new mindset, and new belief. Regardless of your age and regardless of your past, now is the time for you to be new. Now is the time for you to be restored and released.

You don't have to make it a big deal. You don't have to make a big announcement and tell others about it. It's not about other people – it's about you, your life, and your story. Make the decision within your mind and within your heart that you are new. That's what God wants for you. Some of you have been stuck in your current situation long enough. You have been stuck and unable to resume with life after that heartbreaking situation happened, but today things are changing.

The chrysalis is a symbol of isolation and separation. A caterpillar forms a covering that encloses their head and body as their body tissue breaks down and wings, legs and other parts are formed. Butterflies don't die in their cocoon – their whole body transforms. Other insects may call it death, but it's the set up for the greatest breakthrough the butterfly has ever seen.

Your transformation is coming. If you've been in a season of separation and God has been leading you and guiding you through healing and wholeness, get ready for your next stage to be revealed. For a butterfly, when they're in the chrysalis, they don't move. As a human, we have the option to run and hide when things get too hard. We have the choice to quit or give up. Sometimes, our chrysalis season is longer than it should be because we were unfaithful to God. As you enter into your new season, you have to say no more running. Lock in with God so He can finish the work He started. Emerge and become the full butterfly you were meant to be.

Anytime someone sees a butterfly, they see it with bright and beautiful colors. Honestly, I think it's the most unique insect that exists. But just like a butterfly, beautiful and unique with creative colors, that's how God sees you. You've been through things. You've gone through a transformation. You have changed. Now is the time for you to breathe, release, and fly. Here's why: when a butterfly reaches the adult stage and emerges out of the chrysalis, their goal is to go and reproduce. They mate with other butterflies and lay eggs. Some butterflies travel to different continents. This is why we have many varieties of butterflies all throughout the world.

What does that mean for you? When you emerge from your hiding place and fly with freedom, your assignment is to go and tell others about the journey that you have experienced. When your testimony is complete, it's time to share it. That is what creates a seed in other people for them to begin their journey. All of it brings glory to The One who made it all possible. Jesus is the one who saves and sets the captives free. Regardless of your breaking point, you ran to the arms of a loving Savior who transformed your life. Your story will do that for other people. Therefore, spread your wings and fly.

ITS TIME TO DREAM AGAIN

If you had a blank page, where you could dream about anything and you were guaranteed to achieve it, what would those things be? If you had an endless supply of money and you could do whatever you wanted, what would you do?

When you were a little kid, you had dreams like this. You dreamed about things you saw on television. You dreamed about things you heard were possible. You dreamed so much, your eyes lit up when you talked about it. You dreamed and you believed. But as you grew up, people tore them down and said negative things to you. Their words were mean and ruthless and they caused you to think you couldn't accomplish those dreams. Sometimes it was unintentional. Sometimes it wasn't. But your light on the inside went out. You lost your voice. You lost your fire. You lost yourself. Then, instead of dreaming, you became like the people around you. You live in the same area your family lives in, and work jobs like your parents worked. All the while, there is a life on the inside of you that you want to accomplish. There's a tug deep within that you can no longer ignore. This is something that you used to dream about, but when it came time to create a strategy and plan for it, you didn't do it. Or you created the plan and didn't follow it. You didn't have the momentum or the ambition.

God is giving you a new beginning so you can pick that thing back up. It's time to start again. As you connect with your spirit, and allow God to have access to your whole heart, you'll have the freedom to return to these dreams. Not only that, but you'll have the faith to believe and achieve your dreams. The dreams you thought were dead and gone will come back up. God will remind you in your prayer time. God will speak to you randomly throughout the day. You will not be able to ignore what He has placed in your spirit. Just like Jesus had the power to rise from the grave, the God-given dreams that were dead in you will rise again. The hearts that were shattered from all the hurt and pain you went through will be mended back together as if it were brand new. Friendships and family relationships will be restored and better than before. That is the power of beginning again. If you remember in the section Journey to Wholeness, we talked about the beginning when God created Adam and Eve. Although sin corrupted God's plan, Jesus restored it all. When God gives you a new beginning, He is giving you the thing He always wanted you to have.

That was the whole reason for this book. The purpose was to remind you that the best part of your journey is to go back to the beginning – the place you were always supposed to be, where bold and creative ideas came out of you and negative words didn't stop you. The negative words and heartbreaking experiences are going to continue to happen. We live in a fallen world and everybody hasn't taken the time to experience healing like you. The only difference is now you have the tools to overcome the challenges and obstacles that used to stand in your way. When you face the giant this time, you're going to open your heart and process your emotions with God. Through prayer, connecting with your spirit, and spending time with God, you have tools that are more powerful than a sling shot.

You are new. You are healed. You are whole. Start speaking things like this. People are going to notice the changes in your life. They're going to ask you what happened or how you did it? Tell them that God made you new. He took your heart of stone and gave you a heart of flesh. He healed every part of you. Then invite them to experience a new beginning also.

The best part of wholeness is the completion that God provides. James 1:4 says that once patience has its perfect work in you, you will be perfect and complete. That is wholeness. It doesn't mean you won't experience challenges anymore. It means that you don't allow them to have the victory. You have the skills and wisdom to overcome. You won't back down and run away. You have faith to fight back.

Think about this for a second. If you were to accomplish your dreams, encourage others to accomplish theirs and give God praise because He made it all possible; don't you think the enemy would try to stop you? The enemy doesn't want more people to know about God. He is going to do all that he can to slow you down. The good news is that he can't beat you because you're covered by the blood of Jesus. He is already defeated.

As I bring this book to a close, and you prepare to start, or continue, your journey, I want to make sure a few things are clear. There are two ways you can experience a new beginning. Number one is spiritually. That's when you accept Jesus as your Lord and Savior and your spirit becomes one with His Spirit. That is the gift of salvation. Jesus said, I am the way, the truth, and the life, no one comes to the father except by me.

If you haven't accepted Jesus as Lord, now is a great time to do so. Salvation is the first and most important step to experiencing the new things God has in store for you. If you aren't saved, no matter how much you want these things, you don't have access. Jesus is the key. So if you want to receive your new beginning, all you have to do is declare and believe. Declare that Jesus is Lord and believe with your heart that God raised Him from the dead. According to Romans 10:9, that's all it takes. As we mentioned before, to believe something within your heart, leads to changes with your actions. Just believe.

The second way to experience a new beginning is mentally. Wherever your mind goes, your body will follow. Your thoughts, beliefs, and attitudes are the breeding ground for everything you do. You can make a decision today that you don't want to think about the same things. If you want to go to the next level within your career, your goals, your education, your family etc., change your mind.

Philippians 4:8 KJV "Finally, brethren, whatsoever things are true, whatsoever things are honest, whatsoever things are just, whatsoever things are pure, whatsoever things are lovely, whatsoever things are of good report; if there be any virtue, and if there be any praise, think on these things."

Change what you think about. If this is a challenge for you, go on a 21 day fast. Tell yourself that you're only going to watch things that are true, honest, just, pure, lovely and of good report. That means you may have to turn off the news or turn off the reality tv shows. Stop scrolling on Facebook and TikTok. Listen to podcasts. Listen to sermons on YouTube. Fill your ears with positive things for 21 days. Get connected with people who are doing the things you want to do someday. That may be boring. It may be a challenge, but your ears need to hear the change.

Change what you say. Some of this will come naturally as you change what you hear and some of it will require work to implement. Stop saying negative things about yourself and your situation. Speak positively. Even if you don't do anything else, it is scientifically proven that speaking positively can change your situation. The Bible said life and death are in the power of the tongue. What you speak matters. Take some time and start speaking what you want to see.

If you have done these things, my next piece of advice for you is to turn the page. You know how when you're reading a good book and you come to the end of page one, you can't wait to get to page two. Thats how God feels about the story of your life. He already knows what's on the next page, and He wants to reveal it to you. Turn the page and experience the next thing God wants to do in you.

Sometimes people go through hard things and they try to run from it. They run before the page is complete. God doesn't want that. That doesn't lead to growth. It leads to a pause or stagnation. As soon as you stop running, you have to pick back up where you left off. When you're truly healed, you don't run from anything – you walk over it, with God leading and guiding you, He'll make your journey so sweet that you walk over every pitfall and mistake. People will be amazed at how you handle and process the situations. It will all be because of God. God will give you a new page. It'll be a page that's blank and full of unknowns, but that is a good sign that the previous chapter is over. It's complete. You don't have to go backwards, unless you want to reflect on what God did and how He brought you out. Go forward. Heal. It's almost time to turn the page and celebrate the new things that God has in store for you.

THIS IS NOT AN ENDING

A new chapter is upon us as the old chapter closes. This is not an ending – this is a beginning. I thought about all the ways I could conclude this book and I realized, the purpose is to teach you how to begin something new. There is a light available to you every day; you just have to find it and walk in it. It may be hard to find, but you can do it. These words aren't meant to be motivational. These are real things that you can apply to your life. Look at what is on the inside of you – your gifts and talents, your dreams and desires. Imagine you were holding them in your hand. Allow those things to be a light that leads and guides your journey, no matter what life throws your way. You have everything you need to succeed and tackle the next battle.

Initially I picked up my pen and started writing because I was broken and trying to heal from a toxic relationship. Today, I write because I am happy, healed and whole and I want the world to experience this type of freedom. I live life on a new level and it feels good to live in this place.

I'm surrounded by security, support and fulfillment in Christ. I'm happy! This is my journey and I know it's only the beginning. There are many more adventures and experiences waiting on the other side of my obedience. I just have to go and do it.

I pray that you get to experience the wholeness and healing that you desire. Now is your moment. It's your turn to go through your hard situations and lean on God to guide you through it. I hope the stories within this book taught you how to ask yourself the hard questions and allow the Holy Spirit to reveal His words to you. Whatever painful things arise, go through it, smash into your breaking points, and experience your supernatural breakthrough. It won't be hard because you have more than enough tools to lighten the load on your way. Take those steps and move forward. You will not regret it.

One last thing as you go… when one journey ends, another one begins. I will see you in the next chapter.

SCRIPTURE REFERENCES

New Beginnings

Isaiah 43:18-19 Forget the former things; do not dwell on the past. See, I am doing a new thing! Now it springs up; do you not perceive it? I am making a way in the wilderness and streams in the wasteland.

2 Corinthians 5:17 Therefore, if anyone is in Christ, the new creation has come: The old has gone, the new is here!

Ephesians 4:22-24 You were taught, with regard to your former way of life, to put off your old self, which is being corrupted by its deceitful desires; to be made new in the attitude of your minds; and to put on the new self, created to be like God in true righteousness and holiness

Revelations 21:5 He who was seated on the throne said, "I am making everything new!" Then he said, "Write this down, for these words are trustworthy and true."

Salvation

Romans 10:9 If you declare with your mouth, "Jesus is Lord," and believe in your heart that God raised him from the dead, you will be saved.

Love

Romans 5:8 But God demonstrates his own love for us in this: While we were still sinners, Christ died for us.

1 John 4:8-9 Whosoever does not love does not know God, because God is love. This is how God showed his love

among us: He sent his one and only son into the world that we might live through him.

John 3:16 For God so loved the world that he gave his one and only Son, that whoever believes in him shall not perish but have eternal life.

The Heart

1 Samuel 16:7 But the Lord said to Samuel, "Do not consider his appearance or his height, for I have rejected him. The Lord does not look at the things people look at. People look at the outward appearance, but the Lord looks at the heart.

Jeremiah 17:9-10 The heart is deceitful above all things and beyond cure. Who can understand it? I, the Lord, search the heart and examine the mind, to reward each person according to their conduct, according to what their deeds deserve.

Ezekiel 36:26 I will give you a new heart and put a new spirit in you; I will remove your heart of stone and give you a heart of flesh.

Proverbs 4:23 Above all else, guard your heart, for everything you do flows from it.

The Spirit

Romans 8:6 The mind governed by the flesh death, but the mind governed by the Spirit is life and peace.

John 14: 26 But the Advocate, the Holy Spirit, whom the Father will send in my name, will teach you all things and will remind you of everything I have said to you.

10 DAY DEVOTIONAL

EXPERIENCING NEW BEGINNINGS EVERY DAY

As a sweet little treat, I've included this 10- Day Devotional for you to start, or continue, your journey to new beginnings, and build a deeper relationship with God. In this devotional, you will practice giving God your heart, releasing your emotions, and embracing the new things available each day. Each devotional is your opportunity to identify things that may be lingering in your heart, and have an encounter with the unshakeable, relentless love of God that wants you to be free. Read with a heart that truly believes in God and you will encounter his unshakeable presence. As you begin day one, start with a deep breath, and release it slowly.

DAY 1
STAY COMMITTED
— ∞ —

Proverbs 16:3 "Commit to the Lord whatever you do, and he will establish your steps."

Message:

When you submit your actions to God, He orders your steps. God will give you play-by-play instructions of what you're supposed to do. He speaks to you through dreams, other people, and, of course, the word of God. He loves you so much, He doesn't want you to do things on your own. He wants to lead you where you're supposed to be. As a child of God, your number one job is to listen and stay committed to Him.

This is easy to do when everything makes sense, and life turns out the way you thought it would. It's equally important when God is leading you to do something that doesn't make sense. Whatever you do, rely on the scripture because that's what God honors.

Reflection: Ask yourself …

What things do I need to surrender to God today?

What areas of my life am I holding on to and unsure how to release?

Prayer:

Holy Spirit, I ask you to reveal truth to me. If there are things that I'm holding on to, I want to release them, right now. As I breathe in and release the air in my lungs, I take this time to release the thoughts, beliefs and mindsets that aren't pleasing to you. I am enough because your word says it. I am wonderfully and fearfully made. I am yours. I release any lie that tries to tell me otherwise. Amen.

DAY 2
REST IN GOD

—— ∞ ——

Psalms 91:1 "Whoever dwells in the shelter of the Most High will rest in the shadow of the Almighty."

Message:

Where are you resting? Are you resting in God's peace and comfort or in the peace and comfort of your situation? You can rest physically, mentally and emotionally in God. His rest is for every part of you. This is possible when you live a life that dwells with Him. Through your personal relationship with God, He will comfort and protect you better than anyone or anything else. He comforts your mind when anxious thoughts arise. He comforts you emotionally when your feelings are all over the place. As you spend time with God today, remember that He is eternal and your situations are temporary. Rest in God and you will experience the safety that comes with it.

Reflection:

Think about all the things that happened today that caused you to be sad, overwhelmed and distraught. Write them down and release them to the Lord. Take your time as you process and give it to God today.

Prayer:

Dear God, thank you for loving me. In every season and situation, I know you are there. I release the thoughts that are hurting me and keeping me stuck. I release the pain that is living in my heart and I lay it at your feet. As I breathe each breath, I rest in you. In Jesus' name. Amen.

DAY 3
CONTROL YOUR MIND
— ∞ —

Colossians 3:1-2 "Since then, you have been raised with Christ, set your hearts on things above, where Christ is seated at the right hand of God. Set your minds on things above, not on earthly things."

Message:

Every day you have the opportunity to think positively or think negatively. Which one will you choose today? Your thoughts are the beginning of your actions. When you think on things that are faith based and full of scripture, you will find yourself doing things that align with it. Anytime a negative thought comes into your mind, replace it with a positive thought. You have the power to control your mind. Don't allow your thoughts to control you. Meditate on scriptures that help you overcome the negative thoughts and ask Holy Spirit to teach you to control your mind.

Reflection:

Take a moment and examine the thoughts going through your mind. What are some things you thought about earlier? Release and let them go, so you can hear from God in this intimate time. Write down 3 ways you can maintain a positive mindset all throughout your day.

Prayer:

Dear God, I welcome you into this moment and I pause in your presence. I'm thankful that you are seated in heaven and you have given me the victory over my thoughts. Today, I'm making a decision that I'm going to think about things that are pure, righteous, and noble. I am going to align my thoughts with the Spirit and think about things that glorify you. When I face obstacles and challenges, I will keep my mind on things above and I ask your Spirit to remind me when my thoughts wander and drift toward ungodly things. In Jesus' name, Amen

DAY 4
BE GRATEFUL

— ∞ —

1 Thessalonians 5:16-18 "Rejoice Always. Pray continually, give thanks in all circumstances, for this is God's will for you in Christ Jesus"

Message:

Thankfulness is something we can participate in daily. Every day there is a reason to be thankful. When things are hard, being thankful will shift your mood and remind you of the blessings that are right in front of you. Gratefulness reminds you to slow down, be still, and acknowledge God's presence.

Reflection:

Write a list of 10 things you're grateful for. Nothing is too big and nothing is too small.

1.

2.

3.

4.

5.

6.

7.

8.

9.

10.

When you pray, acknowledge these things and give God thanks for each one. If you're asking for something specific, be grateful for where you are currently in life. When the time is right, the Lord will lead you to something new.

Prayer:

Write your own prayer based on the things you're grateful for.

_____

_____

_____

_____

_____

_____

DAY 5
DILIGENT WORKER

—— ∞ ——

Colossians 3:23 "Whatever you do, work at it with all your heart, as working for the Lord"

Message:

As a child, teenager, young adult or older adult – if you're still living on this earth, there is an assignment for you. There is something for you to do with your life. It's easy to get into a rhythm and feel like life is meaningless. But the meaning is in you and the tasks you complete. Your skills and talents are needed. However, the things you do are less important than the way you do it.

Do you work with a heart of excellence? Or do you work with a heart of complaining? God is looking at the posture of your heart. He sees your attitude. Always remember, when you work, you're working for God, not people. Work diligently unto Him and accomplish the assignments He has given you.

Reflection:

How is your attitude today? Take a moment to listen, reflect, and evaluate yourself.

What else do you feel in your spirit that you haven't brought to the Lord? Take a few deep breaths, clear your head, and release these things to God.

Prayer:

Dear God, teach me to be diligent as I am faithful to complete the work you have for me. God, you are my ultimate supervisor, and you see everything I do. Examine my heart, reveal my attitude, and teach me how to work for you. I want you to be satisfied with the assignments I complete. I want you to get glory. Therefore, I surrender my heart and my hands to you. In Jesus' name. Amen.

DAY 6
I AM SAFE

— ∞ —

Ezekiel 36:26 "A new heart also will I give you, and a new spirit will I put within you: and I will take away the stony heart out of your flesh, and I will give you a heart of flesh."

Message:

When a heart is stony, it cannot receive the things of God. It can't even hear or understand it. Is that you? Is your heart cold and calloused? Life may have knocked you down and caused you to become over-protective in an attempt to keep yourself safe. God's hand is gentle. You don't have to protect yourself from Him. He wants to lead and guide you to make you new. Give Him access to your heart and allow Him to do the work to change whatever He wants to change. You are safe in His hands.

Reflection:

Take a moment to pause and think about your life. Draw a picture of what's hiding in your heart. It could be words, phrases or icons – whatever you believe is in you that you haven't been able to share with others. Ask Holy Spirit to reveal truth and show you things that you have never seen before. This is what healing looks like!

Prayer:

Dear God, I ask you to open my eyes and allow me to see what's hiding in my heart. Show me *me*. Take the blinders off my eyes and allow me to see. I thank you for loving me, even the dark places within me, and now I ask you to be the light and help me eradicate everything that's not like you. In Jesus' name I pray, Amen.

DAY 7
BE PURE

— ∞ —

Psalms 51:10 "Create in me a clean heart, oh God; And renew a right spirit within me."

Message:

A clean heart represents purity. Today, you have an opportunity to experience purity within your thoughts, your attitude, and your beliefs. You don't have to think about the same things that you used to think about. God wants you to be clean and that starts with your heart. Will you allow God to renew you? As He moves in your heart and purifies your spirit you will experience everything He wants to give you. There is no need to be ashamed or embarrased of what He may find. He just wants you.

Take a moment to breathe and connect with the living God. He is right here with you. Every breath you take and every breath you release, imagine yourself sitting with God. Be still for a moment. Rest and allow Him to speak with you.

Reflection:

As you spend time with God, take note of what He reveals to you. Are there any words, phrases or images that appear? If so, write it in your journal or on a blank page within this book. Sit with God as long as you need. Then, when you're ready get up and declare that you are pure.

Prayer:

Thank you for this new beginning that you are doing in me. I am redeemed, restored and pure in your sight. As you continue to speak, I am listening. In Jesus' name, Amen.

DAY 8
GIVE PRAISE

—— ∞ ——

Psalms 34 :1 "I will extol the Lord at all times; His praise will always be on my lips."

Message:

What is your favorite scripture? Your favorite can be used to give praise to God. It can be used to fight against the lies of the enemy. The word of God can be applied to your daily life and used to help you become successful with everything you go through. Make a commitment to praise God all throughout your day today. Using songs, scriptures and other expressions of grattitude, praise the Lord. Praise Him with your actions. Praise Him with your thoughts. You will have the victory over every attack when you give praise.

Reflection:

What battles are you fighting today, or this week?

Are you fighting with friends, family or strangers?

Today is the day that God has given you victory. Declare this over ever battle you encounter and believe it. You are victorious in Christ. You can overcome.

Prayer:

Dear God, thank you for giving me the victory. I will praise you today and every day, regardless of what my situation looks like. I praise you because I know you're in control. I know you have won it all. Thank you for being here with me, in this moment and all throughout my day. In Jesus' name, Amen.

DAY 9
TRUST THE LORD

—— ∞ ——

Proverbs 3:5-6 "Trust in the Lord with all your heart and lean not on your own understanding. Acknowledge Him in all your ways and He will make your paths straight."

Message:

Can you trust God when life doesn't make sense and situations don't look the way you want? Trust isn't an easy task when you have your own ideas, expectations and desires. God will make your path straight when you trust Him instead of relying on your understanding. To trust in the Lord means you put His will and His word above your desires and your wants. When you trust God you understand that His ways are better. His ways are wiser. What He wants for you is the best option. If you want to live a life that is successful it's important to trust God with your whole heart.

Reflection:

What dreams and desires do you have?

Do you believe God can make it happen?

What areas of your life are you not trusting God?

What do you need to surrender to God?

Take a few moments to release these things to God as you spend time in prayer.

Prayer:

Dear God, I take this time to surrender to you. I want my dreams to come true and I understand that your word is a promise to making that happen. So, I will trust in you and I will surrender everything to you. Will you search my heart and reveal the pieces of me that are still struggling to trust and believe? In Jesus' name, Amen.

DAY 10
IDENTITY IN CHRIST
— ∞ —

Philippians 4:13 "I can do all things through Christ who strengthens me."

Message:

Do you realize who you are? You were created with a purpose and created in the image of God. Your goals, dreams, and ideas are great. If you're not achieving your dreams, ask yourself why not. Maybe you stopped believing they were possible for you. Maybe you stopped caring about them. Dreams were given to you by God, therefore, it glorifies Him when you are obedient. God will strengthen you when life becomes busy and will remind you to do what He called you to do. Your dreams are a part of your identity, so remember who you are and accomplish your dreams.

Reflection:

Write down 3 statements, starting with I am, to describe who you are. I am _____.

What will you do with the new opportunities, new choices, and new blessings that are available to you today?

Prayer:

Dear God, I embrace this new day. I choose to do things differently and make choices that are different than the previous day. Instead of holding on to unforgiveness our release every situation from my past. I look forward to what this day has to offer and I continue to press on toward the mark that you have set before me. In Jesus' name, Amen.

NOTES

Intro to Wholeness

1. "Damaged Tree Roots" University of Maryland Extension February 27, 2023 https://extension.umd.edu/resource/damaged-tree-roots/

2. "How To Tell If a Tree Is Rotten Inside" Act Tree Service, https://acetreeservice.co/2023/11/30/how-to-tell-if-tree-is-rotten-inside/#:~:text=The%20Main%20Types%20of%20Tree,leading%20to%20decay%20and%20death

A Butterfly in Flight

1. Davis Family Butterfly Vivarium, "Butterfly Metamorphosis" American Museum of Natural History https://www.amnh.org/exhibitions/butterflies/metamorphosis

2. "Butterfly Life Cycle" The Academy of Natural Sciences of Drexel University https://ansp.org/exhibits/online-exhibits/butterflies/lifecycle/#:~:text=The%20butterfly%20and%20moth%20develop,about%204%20or%205%20times

ABOUT THE AUTHOR

Kanisha is a speaker, author and founder of DreamGirls Ministry, with a passion to empower teen girls to achieve their dreams. Born and raised in Duncan, South Carolina, Kanisha has always dreamed big dreams. College was one of the first times she experienced hardship and felt like her dreams weren't possible.

As a student at Gardner-Webb University, Kanisha almost dropped out when she encountered financial hardship. Through hard work, support from family, and guidance from mentors, Kanisha graduated in 2015 with a degree in Journalism and Public Relations. During this season, Kanisha learned how to use faith and hard work to experience success. Now she teaches DreamGirls to do the same thing.

DreamGirls Ministry was founded in June 2014. Its mission is to educate and empower girls to experience the love of Jesus and share it with others. The vision is to be a community of resources to help young girls accomplish their dreams. The organization has grown and expanded in many ways since it's establishment, but the purpose remains the same. They teach people to follow God and follow their dreams. Visit www.dreamgirlsministry.org to learn more about the amazing things this ministry is accomplishing and follow DreamGirls Ministry on social media.

In the face of hardship and opposition, some people quit – Kanisha believes in perseverance. She developed her passion, and God helped her to develop her voice. She speaks boldly and courageously as she educates and empowers others to follow God and follow their dreams. Philippians 4:13 is one of her favorite scriptures and it is the anchor scripture for this ministry.

When she isn't serving in ministry or working, you may

find Kanisha exploring a different country and enjoying this beautiful world God created. Kanisha is a content creator and travel writer, so follow her on all social media platforms and visit the DreamGirls website to read her travel blog. Hopefully through Kanisha's eyes and adventures you will not only see her light but also discover yours.

YouTube: @KanishaBernice
Instagram: @KanishBernice
Facebook: @KanishaBernice

DreamGirls Ministry
Website: www.dreamgirlsministry.org
Instagram: @dreamgirlsministry
Facebook: @dreamgirlsministry

www.ingramcontent.com/pod-product-compliance
Lightning Source LLC
Chambersburg PA
CBHW071628140626
46555CB00021B/1248